CURIOUS Questions and Answers About...

Epic Explorers

Words by Simon Adams

Illustrations by Elissambura

We're curious too, and we want to find out about YOU!
What's your NAME?

How OLD are you?

Where do you live on planet Earth?

What activity do you do for fun?

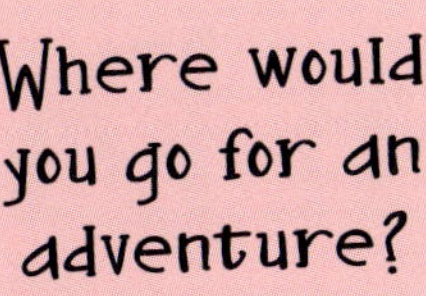

Where would you go for an adventure?

What's your favorite animal?

Who is your best friend?

If you could eat one food every day what would it be?

What's the longest journey you've ever been on?

When Did People Start Exploring?

The first people lived in Africa and began to explore the rest of the world about 200,000 years ago. By 10,000 years ago humans had settled in most parts of the world.

Which queen found a magical land?

In around 1490 BCE **Queen Hatshepsut** of ancient Egypt sent ships across the Red Sea to find new people to trade with. They reached a land called Punt (probably Somalia in East Africa) and returned with precious things never seen before.

Who brought back tales of the midnight Sun?

In around 320 BCE, the Greek sailor **Pytheas** headed north from the Mediterranean. He saw the frozen Arctic Ocean, and described a land where the Sun never set in summer.

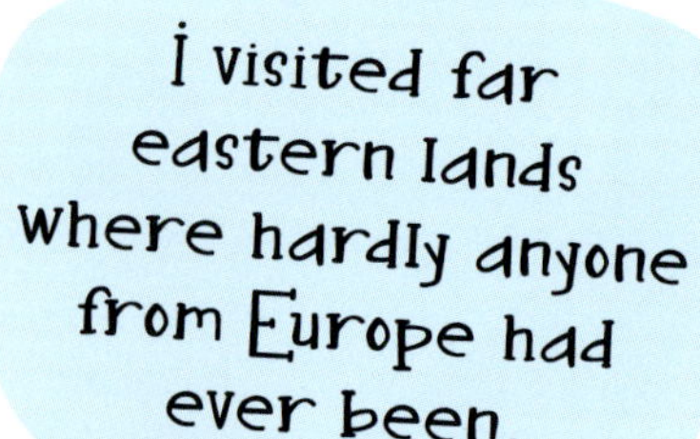

Was the Silk Road Made of Silk?

No – it was named for the Chinese silk that was carried along it to be traded in Europe. In 1271, Italian merchant **Marco Polo** traveled the Silk Road route from Venice to China.

How did ice cream get to Italy?

Some people say the idea was brought back by **Marco Polo** after he learned about similar desserts on his travels in China.

Who went on their dream journey?

Early explorer **Ibn Battuta** left his home in North Africa in 1325 and journeyed throughout Africa and Asia, supposedly after having a dream that a giant bird picked him up and carried him far away.

Whose junk was full of treasure?

Chinese admiral **Zheng He's**. In 1405, he set out on the first of seven major voyages around the Indian Ocean, sailing in a fleet of huge trading ships known as junks.

Did You Know?

British Victorian explorer **Isabella Bird** was also a talented photographer who recorded tales of her travels that amazed the public back at home.

On a trip to Sumatra in 1292, **Marco Polo** was on the hunt for unicorns. Instead, he saw a rhinoceros, and thought he had found one.

American explorer **Hiram Bingham** brought the forgotten Inca city of Machu Picchu in the Andes mountains to world attention in 1911.

American mountaineer **Annie Smith Peck** placed a flag that said "Votes for Women" on the top of Mount Coropuna in Peru in 1911.

British explorer **Gertrude Bell** helped to create the state of Iraq in 1921 after the collapse of the Ottoman Empire.

Alaska's Admiralty Island is home to lots of grizzly bears. It's known as **"Fortress of the Bears"** in the local Tlingit language, and early Russian explorers called it "Fear Island"!

English explorer **Mary Kingsley** bravely traveled alone through West Africa in the 1890s. She fought crocodiles and had three new species of fish named after her.

Mount Disappointment in Australia got its name when two British explorers climbed to the top in 1824 and couldn't see the sea!

Why Isn't Greenland Green?

Because the Viking sailor **Erik the Red** lied about it! Erik traveled to the island around 1000 CE. He found it cold and icy, but named it Greenland to try to get more people to join him.

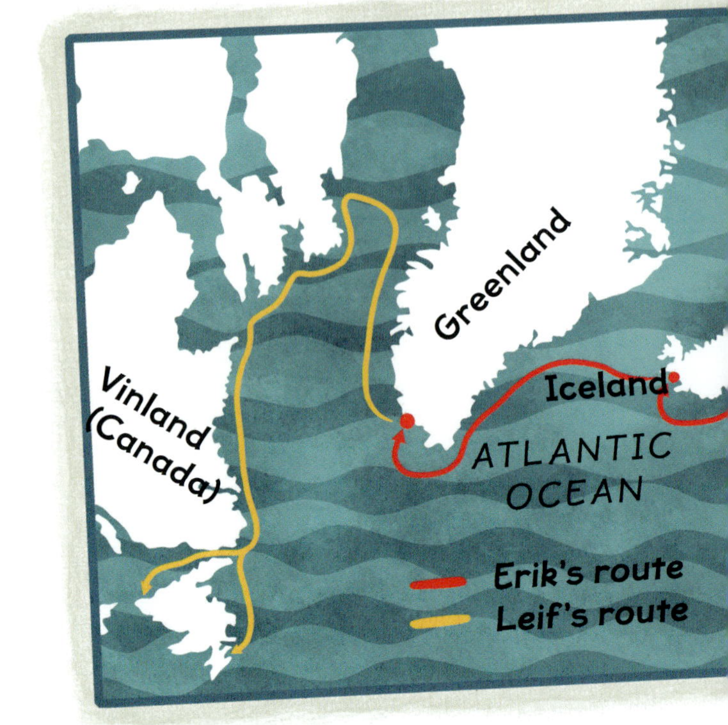

Who visited America but didn't stay?

Erik the Red's son, **Leif Erikson**, and his fellow Vikings explored a place he called Vinland, in modern-day Canada. They founded a new settlement but didn't stay very long before returning to Greenland.

Where did Columbus think he was?

When Italian explorer **Christopher Columbus** landed on an island he named San Salvador in 1492, he thought it was part of Asia. In fact, it was the Bahamas, and he was actually on the continent now called America.

What Was the Age of Exploration?

Europeans started to sail great distances around the globe from the 1480s, in a time we call the Age of Exploration. They made new trade routes and claimed foreign lands.

Who made it easier to get spices?

Portuguese explorer **Vasco da Gama** did when he found a new sea route to India in 1498.

Before then, spices from India and the Far East used to take ages to get to Europe overland.

So, da Gama's discovery made the spice journey much easier.

Who first sailed all around the world?

In 1522, **Juan Sebastián Elcano** returned to Spain after a three-year journey around the globe. He was part of explorer **Ferdinand Magellan's** expedition to find a route west to far eastern Spice Islands. He led the voyage after Magellan died in 1521.

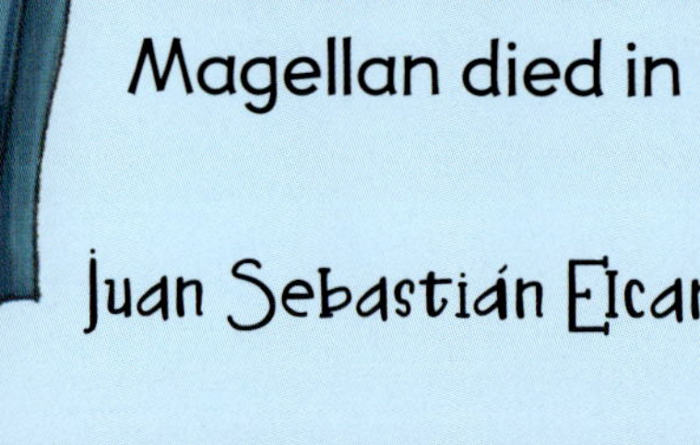

How did Canada get its name?

In 1535, **Jacques Cartier** sailed to North America from France. The local Iroquois people gave him directions to a village, which they called a kanata. Cartier thought the whole region was called kanata, which evolved into the name "Canada."

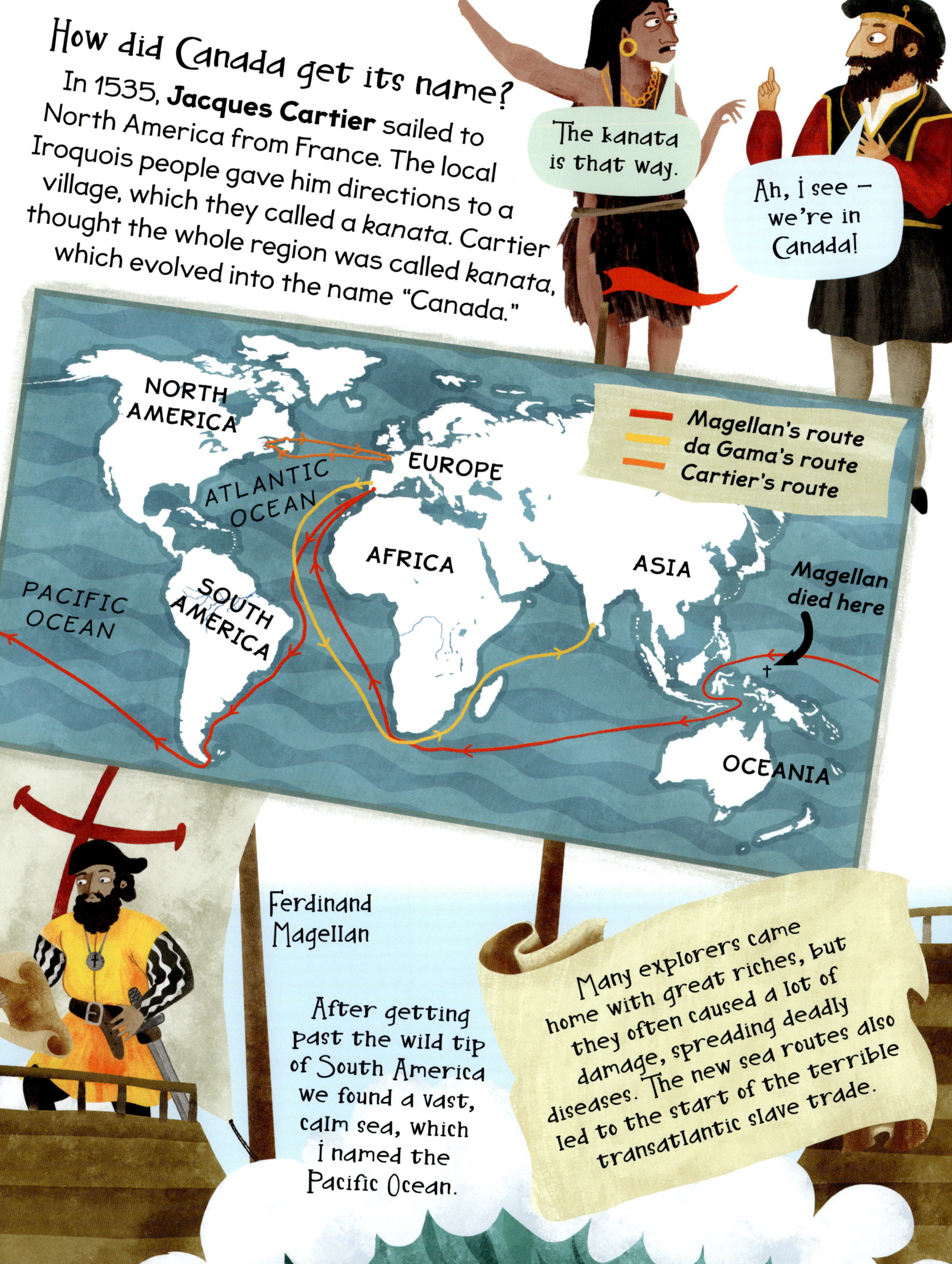

Ferdinand Magellan

After getting past the wild tip of South America we found a vast, calm sea, which I named the Pacific Ocean.

Many explorers came home with great riches, but they often caused a lot of damage, spreading deadly diseases. The new sea routes also led to the start of the terrible transatlantic slave trade.

How Many?

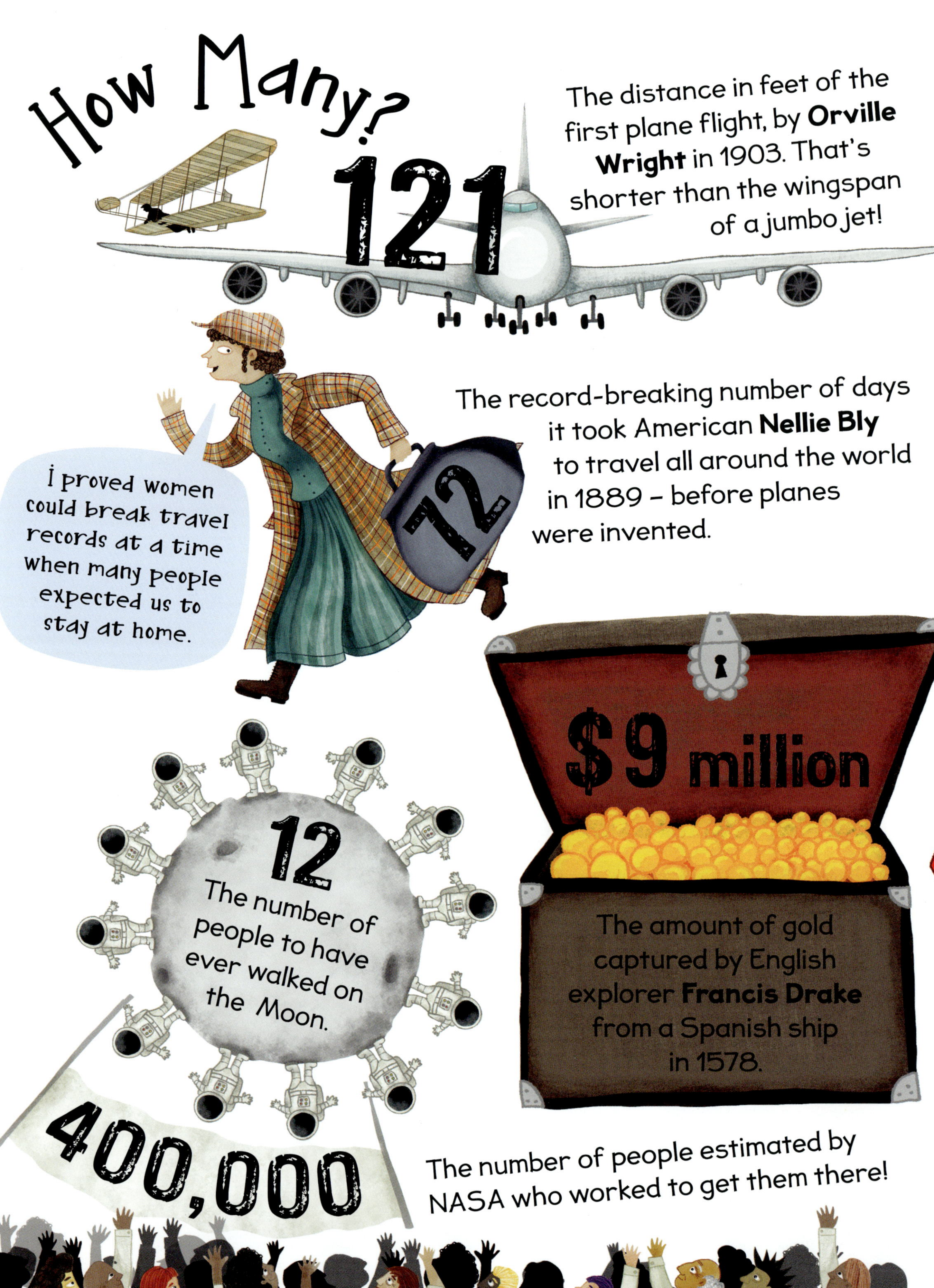

121

The distance in feet of the first plane flight, by **Orville Wright** in 1903. That's shorter than the wingspan of a jumbo jet!

72

The record-breaking number of days it took American **Nellie Bly** to travel all around the world in 1889 – before planes were invented.

12
The number of people to have ever walked on the Moon.

$9 million

The amount of gold captured by English explorer **Francis Drake** from a Spanish ship in 1578.

400,000

The number of people estimated by NASA who worked to get them there!

14

19

The time in days it took British pilot **Amy Johnson** to fly solo from England to Australia in 1930, becoming the first woman to do so.

15

The time in minutes spent on the summit of Mount Everest by **Edmund Hillary** and **Tenzing Norgay**, the first people to climb it in 1953.

149,129

The distance in miles sailed by one of the first female explorers, Austrian **Ida Pfeiffer**, on her travels in the 1840s and 1850s.

14.7 billion

Distance in miles from Earth of the Voyager 1 space probe, which has been exploring the Solar System for 48 years and counting!

Who Sailed in a Coal Boat?

British explorer **James Cook** was chosen to captain a former coal boat, the *Endeavour*, on a journey around the world in 1768. He made two further global voyages, exploring many places that hadn't been mapped.

Cook visited Australia, New Zealand, Tahiti, Hawaii, and even got close to Antarctica, mapping many coastlines along the way.

Who found new plants and animals?

Botanist **Joseph Banks** traveled on Captain Cook's ship *Endeavour*. Banks took advantage of the lands they visited, studying, drawing, and collecting thousands of species.

Who named Australia?

English sailor **Matthew Flinders** gave Australia its name after sailing around it in 1802–1803. He was helped by **Bungaree**, an Aboriginal interpreter and guide who became the first person to be described as an "Australian."

Who sailed around the world in disguise?

French explorer and botanist **Jeanne Baret** did. As a woman, Jeanne wasn't allowed to travel on naval expeditions so, in 1766, she disguised herself as a man, called herself Jean, and set off on a voyage across the globe.

Who Got Sent to Cross America?

President Jefferson sent **Meriwether Lewis** and **William Clark** to explore the newly enlarged United States in 1803. Much of the vast land was unmapped and the two explorers faced many dangers along the way.

Who saved the day?

A young Shoshone woman called **Sacagawea** acted as a translator and guide for Lewis and Clark. She took her newborn baby boy with her, traveling thousands of miles to the Pacific Ocean and back.

How did camels get to Australia?

When Europeans started exploring inland Australia about 200 years ago, they brought camels from India that were used to trekking in very dry conditions.

There are now more than one million wild camels in Australia!

Why was crossing Australia so hard?

Scorching temperatures and scarce water made finding a route across the country very tough. Prize money led different expeditions to attempt it in the 1860s, but some would die trying.

Who Went on African Adventures?

Many European explorers traveled in Africa in the 1800s — a time when there weren't any maps for large parts of the continent. They all wanted to say they had got somewhere "first."

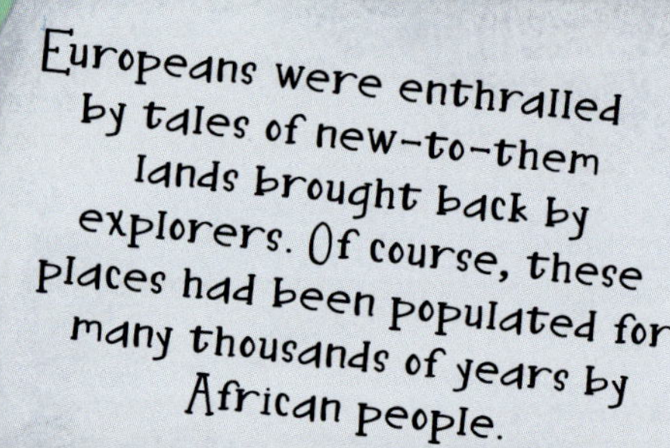

Europeans were enthralled by tales of new-to-them lands brought back by explorers. Of course, these places had been populated for many thousands of years by African people.

Who looked for the source of the Nile?

John Speke and **Richard Burton** trekked many miles looking for the start of the river Nile, which they thought flowed from a lake in the middle of Africa.

Speke named the lake Victoria, after Queen Victoria.

They caught many tropical diseases and were often sick.

Richard got sick and had to stop and rest. John kept going, eventually finding the lake in 1858, becoming the first European to see it.

Where was Livingstone lost?

Famous Victorian explorer **Dr. David Livingstone** went missing in East Africa in the 1860s. He had walked right across Africa, sailed down the Zambezi and was the first European to see the *Mosi-oa-Tunya* waterfall, which he named Victoria Falls.

Livingstone was mauled by a lion on his travels.

Who found him?

Writer and explorer **Henry Stanley** went to look for Livingstone, eventually finding him in Tanzania in 1871.

Who took grand expeditions to the Nile?

Women had few chances to become explorers in the 1800s, but a young Dutch woman, **Alexine Tinné**, threw herself into travel. Along with her mother, she visited the vast area around the Nile river in the 1860s.

David Livingstone said Tinné was the best explorer he knew!

In 1869, Alexine tried to cross the huge Sahara Desert but was sadly killed in a raid.

Would You Rather?

Go exploring in a **plane**...

...or onboard a **sailboat**?

Explore a **baking hot** desert...

Visit unexplored parts of **Earth**...

...or unexplored parts of the **Moon**?

Discover a new **plant**...

Navigate using a map or a phone? (You can't take both!)
Travel the furthest distance...
...or for the longest time?
...or a freezing cold ice cap?
Brrrr!
Spend two months on a mountain climbing expedition...
...or two months onboard a submarine?
Quack!
...or a new animal?
Name a waterfall you discovered after yourself or your pet?
How about "Fido Falls"?
23

Who Got to the North Pole First?

Believe it or not, people have been arguing about this for years! Because the North Pole is in the frozen Arctic ice, it was very hard for explorers to tell if they'd got there or not!

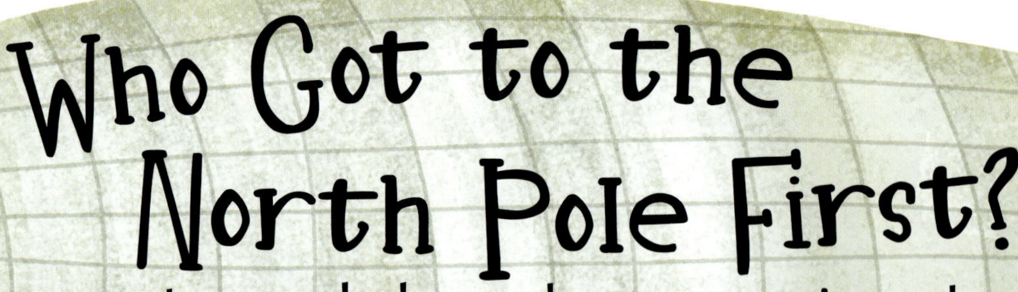

Roald Amundsen (Norwegian)

Robert Peary and Matthew Henson (American)

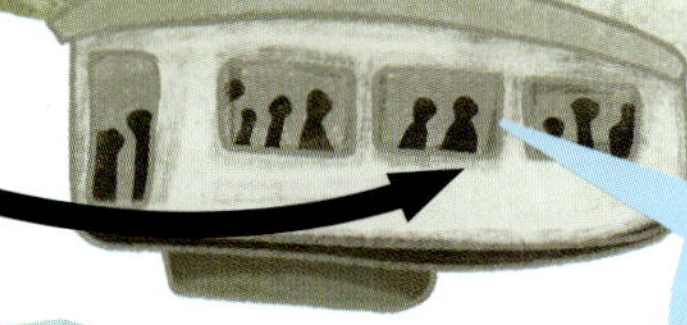

Frederick Cook (American)

How did Jo Peary help?

Jo Peary went on many adventures with her husband Robert at a time when women usually stayed at home. An explorer in her own right, she organized a rescue mission when Robert was stranded on the wrong side of an ice cap!

Who raced to the South Pole?

A Norwegian team, led by **Roald Amundsen**, and a British expedition, led by **Robert Falcon Scott**. Amundsen reached the pole in December 1911 and Scott's team arrived a month later, but died on the return journey.

Who Stood on Top of the World?

On May 29, 1953, New Zealander **Edmund Hillary** and Nepalese mountaineer **Tenzing Norgay** became the first people to climb the 29,032-foot (8,849-m) high Mount Everest in the Himalayas. The world's highest mountain had been conquered at last.

Who climbed Everest – and more?

On May 16, 1975, Japanese mountaineer **Junko Tabei** became the first woman to conquer Everest. In 1992, she then became the first woman to climb the Seven Summits, the highest mountain on each continent. Her motto was...

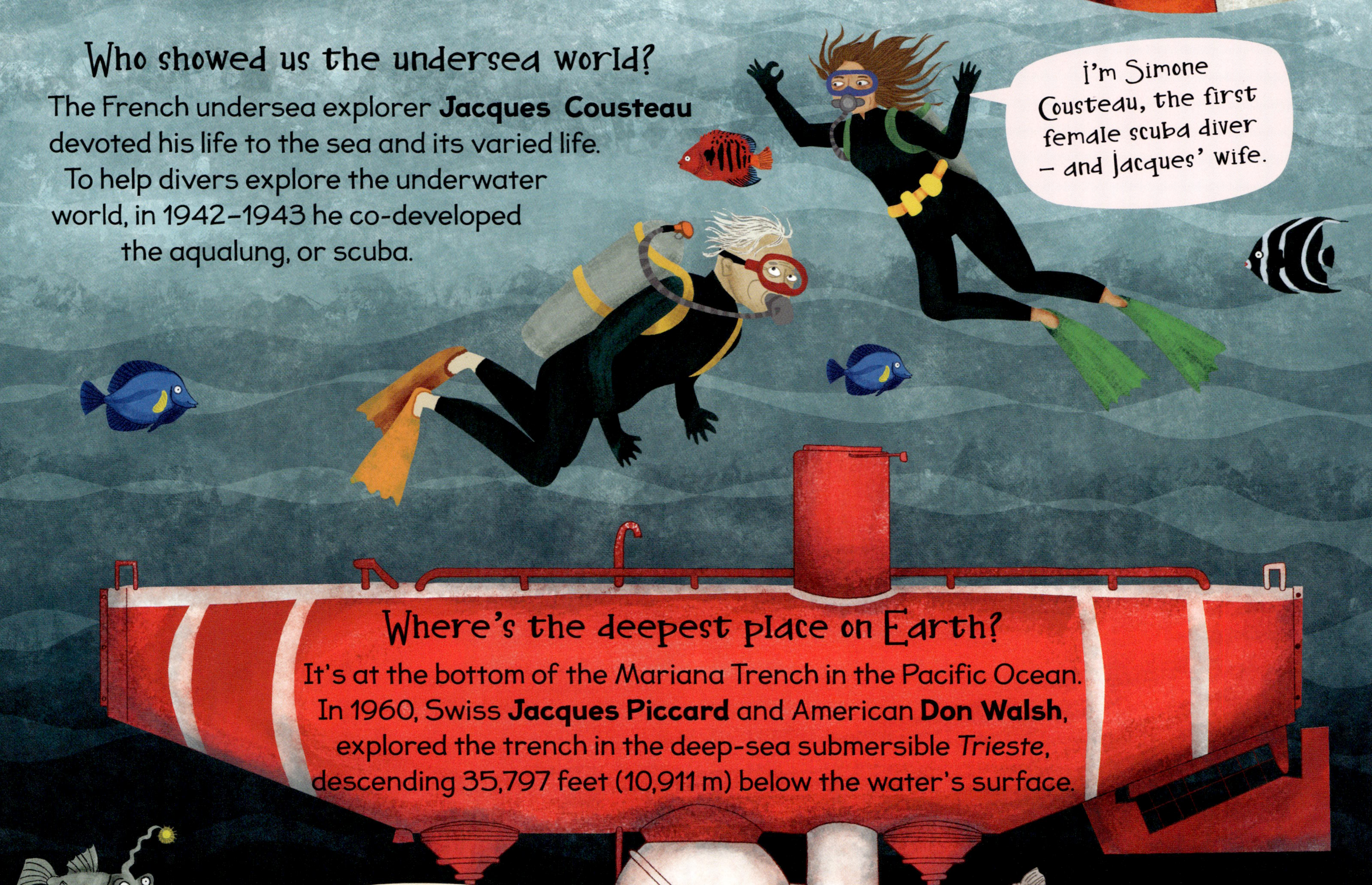

Who showed us the undersea world?

The French undersea explorer **Jacques Cousteau** devoted his life to the sea and its varied life. To help divers explore the underwater world, in 1942–1943 he co-developed the aqualung, or scuba.

Where's the deepest place on Earth?

It's at the bottom of the Mariana Trench in the Pacific Ocean. In 1960, Swiss **Jacques Piccard** and American **Don Walsh**, explored the trench in the deep-sea submersible *Trieste*, descending 35,797 feet (10,911 m) below the water's surface.

Who Was the First Man in Space?

Russian cosmonaut **Yuri Gagarin** blasted off into space on April 12, 1961 in the *Vostok 1* capsule. He whizzed once around the planet before landing back on Earth one hour and 48 minutes later.

Gagarin landed in a potato field, scaring the local villagers.

And who was the first woman?

Valentina Tereshkova became the first woman in space when she orbited Earth, alone, for just under three days in June 1963. She was only 26 years old at the time.

How long did it take to fly to the Moon?

It took 4 days, 6 hours, 45 minutes and 40 seconds for the first people to get to the Moon. After landing, **Neil Armstrong** became the first human to walk on its surface, on July 21, 1969, followed by **Buzz Aldrin**.

Neil, Buzz, and Michael were on NASA's Apollo 11 mission.

A Compendium of Questions

Who never gave up?

Ernest Shackleton was exploring Antarctica in 1914 when his ship got crushed by ice. The crew eventually sailed to a tiny island in lifeboats, then a small group braved terrible seas to get to another island for help.

Who circled the globe?

Epic adventurer **Ranulph Fiennes** traveled from north to south around the poles between 1979 and 1982, without using planes.

Who left his heart behind?

When explorer **David Livingstone** died in 1873, his heart was buried in Africa, while the rest of his body was returned to England.

Where is the Valley of the Assassins?

This legendary place with a ruined medieval fortress is in northern Iran. British-Italian explorer, **Freya Stark**, was the first Westerner to trek to it in 1931.

Who missed Australia?

In 1642, Dutch explorer **Abel Tasman** landed in Van Diemen's Land (now called Tasmania) and reached New Zealand, but sailed right round Australia without noticing it!

Who broke boundaries?

In 1992, doctor and astronaut **Mae Jemison** orbited Earth on the space shuttle *Endeavour*, becoming the first Black woman to travel in space.

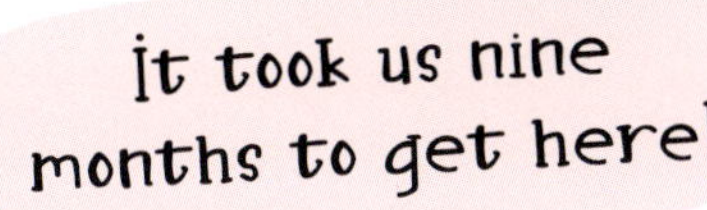

Is there anywhere left to explore?

Yes! Only 20 percent of the world's oceans have been fully explored, and just 5 percent of the seabed.

Will we ever walk on Mars?

Mars has been visited by spacecraft, but it has no breathable air and its surface temperature is below freezing. Despite this, many space agencies are working on plans to send humans to Mars.

Published in 2026 by Windmill Books,
an Imprint of Rosen Publishing
2544 Clinton St.
Buffalo, NY 14224

First published in 2023 by Miles Kelly Publishing Ltd
Copyright © Miles Kelly Publishing Ltd 2023

Publishing Director   Belinda Gallagher
Creative Director   Jo Cowan
Editorial Director   Rosie Neave
Senior Editor   Becky Miles
Designers   Simon Lee, Joe Jones, Karen Doughty
Production   Elizabeth Collins
Reprographics   Stephan Davis
Consultant   Anna Claybourne

Cataloging-in-Publication Data
Names: Adams, Simon, author. | Elissambura, illustrator.
Title: Epic explorers / by Simon Adams, illustrated by Elissambura.
Description: Buffalo, NY : Windmill Books, 2026. | Series: Curious questions and answers about...
Identifiers: ISBN 9781538398982 (pbk.) | ISBN 9781538398999 (library bound) | ISBN 9781538399002 (ebook)
Subjects: LCSH: Discoveries in geography--Juvenile literature. | Explorers--Juvenile literature.
Classification: LCC G175.A336 2026 | DDC 910.92--dc23

CPSIA Compliance Information: Batch #CSWM26
For Further Information contact Rosen Publishing at 1-800-237-9932

Find us on